Living Stones

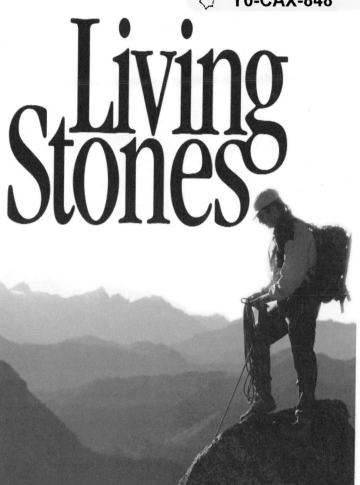

Living Stones

Becoming a Rock-Solid Christian

Richard L Ruth

SYNERGY Publishers
Gainesville, Florida 32614 USA

A division of Bridge-Logos International Trust
in partnership with **Bridge-Logos** *Publishers*

Living Stones

by Richard L. Ruth

International Standard Book Number: 1-931727-01-5
Library of Congress Catalog Card Number: 2001095971

Published by:
Synergy Publishers
Gainesville, Florida USA
SP-7015 Discipleship
www.synergypublishers.com

Synergy Publishers is a division of Bridge-Logos International Trust, Inc., in partnership with Bridge-Logos Publishers.

All these died in faith, without receiving the promises, but having seen them and having welcomed them from a distance, and having confessed that they were strangers and exiles on the earth. For those who say such things make it clear that they are seeking a country of their own. And indeed if they had been thinking of that {country} from which they went out, they would have had opportunity to return. But as it is, they desire a better {country}, that is, a heavenly one. Therefore God is not ashamed to be called their God; for He has prepared a city for them.

Hebrews 11:13–16 NASU

Contents

How to Use this Handbook

Living Stones: Becoming a Rock-Solid Christian is a unique handbook for you to read continually from cover to cover. The closest of its kind is a daily meditation book or a book that takes the reader through the Bible in one year.

Keep reading these powerful Scriptures to become a disciple of Jesus Christ and to train other disciples. This handbook doesn't belong on a shelf!

To the best of my knowledge no other handbook exists to briefly describe the history of salvation through Scripture and then to use only Scripture quotes to show its continued unfolding. I've chosen six popular Bible translations to highlight important Christian concepts. As a believer, you'll understand more clearly your purpose in life and see your individual and joint responsibilities before God.

The handbook is divided into three main parts: History of Salvation, The Resurrection Gift and Laying the Foundation of the kingdom. Special features include *My Notes* pages, for your personal study notes and journal, and the *Salvation Prayer List*.

I invite you to take this guide on your pilgrimage to successful and powerful Christian living.

INTRODUCTION

The call to worship and serve the LORD is real. It is my opinion that it has never been more imperative than in the 21st Century.

We disciples of Jesus Christ of Nazareth need a concise set of scriptural guidelines to work with the Holy Spirit in laying the foundation of the Kingdom. Let's get started today and keep watching for His return.

Joshua, upon entering the Promised Land, faced a great war to establish God's kingdom. We are faced with a task of an even greater dimension in establishing His Kingdom, since our battle is with the unseen spiritual forces of Satan and his minions.

> For though we walk in the flesh, we do not war according to the flesh. For the weapons of our warfare are not of the flesh, but divinely powerful for the destruction of fortresses. {We are} destroying speculations and every lofty thing raised up against the knowledge of God, and {we are} taking every thought captive to the obedience of Christ (2 Corinthians 10:3–5 NASU).

We must be well prepared to do battle and to know for whom, with whom, and how to do battle. We must take a position of either being for or against the setting up of His kingdom. If, as disciples of Jesus Christ of Nazareth, we do not take a position of being for Him, we are, in essence, taking a position against Him.

> To the angel of the church of Laodicea write: The Amen, the faithful and true Witness, the Beginning of the creation of God says this: "I know your deeds, that you are neither cold nor hot; I wish that you were cold or hot. So because you are lukewarm, and neither hot nor cold, I will spit you out of My mouth. Because you say, 'I am rich, and have become wealthy, and have need of nothing,' and you do not know that you are wretched and miserable and poor and blind and naked" (Revelation 3:14–17 NASU).

What Jesus Says

Jesus has already told us that we are in a battle.

> Do not think that I have come to bring peace on the earth; I did not come to bring peace, but a sword (Matthew 10:34 NASU).

> The Son of God appeared for this purpose, to destroy the works of the devil (1 John 3:8b NASU).

The sword we use is not a physical sword, but is the Word of God, that is, Scripture.

> For the word of God is living and active and sharper than any two-edged sword, and piercing as far as the division of soul and spirit, of both joints and marrow, and able to judge the thoughts and intents of the heart (Hebrews 4:12 NASU).

Reaching Out

The first purpose of writing this book was for my own edification. I wanted to write down why I believe in a Creator, His purpose in creating me and how I am to live my life to fulfill that purpose. I wanted a handbook that I could readily refer to on my pilgrimage, a handbook that would always be consistent with the Bible.

Secondly, if I found this handbook to be helpful to me in my decision-making, it might also be helpful to others. I've focused on the Bible's most powerful verses on salvation and the Resurrection. Use this handbook for sharing the Gospel with others. It's also great for personal or group discipleship study. If you're a new believer, I've inserted notes to help you.

Finally, my third purpose is to instill a burning desire to ask the Holy Spirit to assist us daily in the study of the Scriptures and to help us listen to the small, still voice of God. This is how faith, which is a gift from God (Ephesians 2:8 NASU), comes to us (Romans 10:17). If your faith needs a boost, open God's Word at the same time each day and devote yourself to seek answers from Him. The investment you make in God's Kingdom lasts for eternity. Wall Street can't give you that guarantee.

Therefore, since we are surrounded by such a great cloud of witnesses, let us throw off everything that hinders and the sin that so easily entangles, and let us run with perseverance the race marked out for us. Let us fix our eyes on Jesus, the author and perfecter of our faith, who for the joy set before him endured the cross, scorning its shame, and sat down at the right hand of the throne of God (Hebrews 12:1–2 NIV).

Daily Guide

This handbook is divided into three main divisions. In the first part, I share my scriptural understanding of why I believe in God and God's purpose for creating you and I. Some of the scriptures have been annotated with italicized text in square brackets, such as "[*Jesus*]". This text is inserted to clarify the context of the scripture.

You've probably never seen Bible verses on salvation and discipleship one right after the other. Now you have this handbook as a daily reference guide for witnessing, study and most of all, helping others to follow Jesus Christ. The middle section of this handbook contains a Resurrection essay and Scriptures that are powerfully central to our beliefs as disciples of Jesus Christ.

Are you still wondering about God's will for your life? The third part of this book details how to live in order to fulfill God's purpose. Find answers to your questions from these revealing Bible verses. My prayer is that you will be a living stone for Jesus.

Come to Christ, who is the living cornerstone of God's temple. He was rejected by the people, but he is precious to God who chose him. And now God is building you, as living stones, into his spiritual temple. (1 Peter 2:4–5a NLT).

PART I

HISTORY OF SALVATION

PART I

HISTORY OF SALVATION

Meet the Creator

The God of Abraham, Isaac, Jacob, and the God and Father of Jesus Christ, created the earth and everything that is in it as well as the universe through Jesus (John 1:3; Ephesians 3:9; Colossians 1:15–17). In creation He expressed His love, intelligence, and power. All things, therefore, must honor, worship and be obedient to the Creator.

So Paul, standing before the Council addressed them as follows: "Men of Athens, I notice that you are very religious, for as I was walking along I saw your many altars. And one of them had this inscription on it —'To an Unknown God.' You have been worshiping him without knowing who he is, and now I wish to tell you about him. He is the God who made the world and everything in it. Since he is Lord of heaven and earth, he doesn't live in man-made temples, and human hands can't serve his needs—for he has no needs. He himself gives life and breath to everything, and he satisfies every need there is. From one man he created all the nations throughout the whole earth. He decided beforehand which should rise and fall, and he determined their boundaries. His purpose in all of this was that the nations should seek after God and perhaps feel their way toward him and find him though he is not far from any one of us. For in him we live and move and exist" (Acts 17:22–28a NLT).

Road to Salvation

What is absolutely essential to salvation (or the blessing of eternal life)?

Belief and faith in God are essential. First, one must believe in the God who created the heaven and earth (Genesis 1:1). Secondly, one must believe in the God of Abraham, Isaac and Jacob (Exodus 3:6). Finally, one must believe in Jesus Christ and what the Scriptures say about Him (Romans 10: 9–10).

Faith comes by hearing what the Scriptures say about these matters (Romans 10:17). This is not just head faith or mental assent. This is heart faith:

If one loves God truly [with affectionate reverence, prompt obedience, and grateful recognition of His blessing], he is known by God [recognized as

4

worthy of His intimacy and love, and he is owned by Him] (1 Corinthians 8:3 AMP).

For [if we are] in Christ Jesus, neither circumcision nor uncircumcision counts for anything, but only faith activated and energized and expressed and working through love (Galatians 5:6 AMP).

Obviously, anyone who wants to come to Him must believe that there is a God and that He rewards those who sincerely seek Him (Hebrews 11:6 NLT).

None of us have any excuse to doubt the existence of God.

For the wrath of God is revealed from heaven against all ungodliness and unrighteousness of men who suppress the truth in unrighteousness, because that which is known about God is evident within them; for God made it evident to them. For since the creation of the world His invisible attributes, His eternal power and divine nature, have been clearly seen, being understood through what has been made, so that they are without excuse (Romans 1:18–20 NASU).

God's Covenant

Abraham, Moses, and the Prophets began to lay the foundation for the Kingdom that would be inaugurated by Jesus. Our prime example for powerful faith in God is Abraham. He believed God without any reservation—even to the point of sacrificing His only son if God required it.

Now, do you know how a man of faith was identified in the Old Testament?

The sign of those that believed in the God of Abraham was obedience to the circumcision. The obedience to this personal physical sign was followed by physical and spiritual obedience to God's commandments as given through Moses, which included the rituals for worship and the expiation (washing away) of sins.

In those days, God provided forgiveness to men and women through the shedding of the blood of animals.

Significance of Blood of Jesus

God said that life is in the blood (Leviticus 17:11 NLT). He used the shedding of blood as a sign of forgiveness of sins: forgiveness of the original sin of Adam and Eve and the sins of His people in disobedience to His Commandments. Blood was also symbolic in the establishment of His Covenants (Abrahamic, Mosaic, Christian).

The use of the blood in the animal sacrifices under the Mosaic Law came before the shedding of divine blood through His Son, Jesus. This was done as a once-and-for-all sacrificial shedding of His own blood for the forgiveness of mankind's sins against the Creator.

> And so, dear brothers and sisters, we can boldly enter heaven's Most Holy Place because of the blood of Jesus. This is the new, life-giving way that Christ has opened up for us through the sacred curtain, by means of his death for us (Hebrews 10:19–20 NLT).

Jesus himself confirms this:

And he took a cup of wine and gave thanks to God for it. He gave it to them and said, "Each of you drink from it, for this is my blood, which seals the covenant between God and his people. It is poured out to forgive the sins of many" (Matthew 26:27–28 NLT).

It is drunk by believers in remembrance of Him and what His blood has bought for them (1 Corinthians 11:23–26 NLT).

Besides confessing that Jesus is one's Lord and Savior and believing in one's heart that God raised Him from the dead, is there anything else we need to know?

Well, it's necessary to understand what the shedding of Jesus' blood does for believers and to consider what happens to those who ignore this sacrifice:

We are made right with God when we believe that Jesus shed his blood sacrificing his life for us ... (Romans 3:25b NLT).

Anyone who refused to obey the law of Moses was put to death without mercy on the testimony of two or three witnesses. Think how much more terrible the punishment will be for those who have trampled on the Son of God and have treated the blood of the covenant as if it were common and unholy. Such people have insulted and enraged the Holy Spirit who brings God's mercy to his people (Hebrews 10:28–29 NLT).

Resurrection Power

By the shedding of the precious blood of Jesus, His followers, who are called His chosen, receive the indwelling of the Holy Spirit with Resurrection power. The promise of God to Abraham's seed, i.e., to Jesus, and those who believe in Jesus, is specifically the indwelling of the Holy Spirit. The same Holy Spirit who was with Jesus became available to believers in Him at Pentecost. Did you know that it is only by the power of the Holy Spirit that the kingdom of God becomes actively involved in your life and by Whom you are able to withstand the onslaughts of the enemy?

> Christ redeemed us from the curse of the Law, having become a curse for us—for it is written, "CURSED IS EVERYONE WHO HANGS ON A TREE"—in order that in Christ Jesus the blessing of Abraham might come to the Gentiles, so that we would receive the promise of the Spirit through faith (Galatians 3:13–14 NASU).

> Because you are sons [*and daughters*], God has sent forth the Spirit of His Son into our hearts, crying "Abba! Father!" (Galatians 4:6 NASU).

Indwelling of the Holy Spirit

We must have the Holy Spirit dwelling in our hearts in order to live a life pleasing to the Father. The Holy Spirit enables us to do our part in the establishment of His kingdom.

Receive Gifts of the Holy Spirit

God can change our hearts sovereignly as He wishes (see Romans 9 NASU). Everything depends on His mercy. I can, however, make my heart more responsive to the indwelling of the Holy Spirit by accepting Jesus as my Lord and Savior. In addition, I can enhance this indwelling by responding to Him and asking for His wisdom and guidance (Proverbs 3:5–6 NASU).

If my attitude is that of giving and not always trying to get, I become more receptive to the gifts of the Holy Spirit. Constantly trying to *get* from the Father implies that I am depending upon my works. But if I am conscious of giving of myself and of my substance, I am patterning my life after Jesus and the Father and then I become more likely to receive His gifts.

Focus on these four areas to become more responsive and more receptive of the gifts of the Holy Spirit—for the establishment of His kingdom and the strength and power needed to withstand the onslaughts of the enemy: (a) Faith, (b) Obedience, (c) Worship, and (d) Desire.

Faith

> For since the creation of the world His invisible attributes, His eternal power and divine nature, have been clearly seen, being understood through what has been made, so that they [*men who suppress the truth in unrighteousness*] are without excuse (Romans 1:20 NASU).

> And without faith it is impossible to please {Him}, for he who comes to God must believe that He is and {that} He is a rewarder of those who seek Him (Hebrews 11:6 NASU).

> For this Good News—that God has prepared a place of rest—has been announced to us just as it was to them [*Israelites*]. But it did them no good because they didn't believe what God had told them. For only we who believe can enter his place of rest. As for those who didn't believe, God said, "In my anger I made a vow: They will never enter my place of

rest," even though his place of rest has been ready since he made the world (Hebrews 4:2–3 NLT).

Obedience

Samuel said, "Has the Lord as much delight in burnt offerings and sacrifices As in obeying the voice of the Lord? Behold, to obey is better than sacrifice, {And} to heed than the fat of rams. For rebellion is as the sin of divination, And insubordination is as iniquity and idolatry" (1 Samuel 15:22–23a NASU).

For example, in Acts, Jesus Christ told believers to wait for the Holy Spirit to fill them:

Gathering them together, He commanded them not to leave Jerusalem, but to wait for what the Father had promised, "Which," He said, "you heard from Me; for John baptized with water, but you will be baptized with the Holy Spirit not many days from now" (Acts 1:4–5 NASU).

Then they, about 120 persons, went to an upper room where the apostles were staying and devoted themselves to prayer. Being obedient to Jesus' command, the Holy Spirit came and filled them (Acts 2:1–4).

Worship and Desire

God rewards a giver and worshiper of Him with the infilling of the Holy Spirit. Cornelius and his family are a good example:

Now {there was} a man at Caesarea named Cornelius, a centurion of what was called the Italian cohort, a devout man and one who feared God with all his household, and gave many alms to the

{Jewish} people and prayed to God continually. About the ninth hour [*3:00 P.M.*] of the day he clearly saw in a vision an angel of God who had {just} come in and said to him, "Cornelius!" And fixing his gaze on him and being much alarmed, he said, "What is it, Lord?" And he said to him, "Your prayers and alms have ascended as a memorial before God. Now dispatch {some} men to Joppa and send for a man {named} Simon, who is also called Peter."

[*Peter preaches to Cornelius and his household*] "{You know of} Jesus of Nazareth, how God anointed Him with the Holy Spirit and with power, and {how} He went about doing good and healing all who were oppressed by the devil, for God was with Him. We are witnesses of all the things He did both in the land of Jews and in Jerusalem. They also put Him to death by hanging Him on a cross. God raised Him up on the third day and granted that He become visible, not to all the people, but to witnesses who were chosen beforehand by God, {that is}, to us who ate and drank with Him after He arose from the dead. And He ordered us to preach to the people, and solemnly to testify that this is the One who has been appointed by God as Judge of the living and the dead. Of Him all the prophets bear witness that through His name everyone who believes in Him receives forgiveness of sins."

While Peter was still speaking these words, the Holy Spirit fell upon all those who were listening to the message. All the circumcised believers who came with Peter were amazed, because the gift of the Holy Spirit had been poured out on the Gentiles also. For they were hearing them speaking with tongues and exalting God. Then Peter answered, "Surely no one can refuse the water for these to be baptized who have received the Holy Spirit just as we {did}, can he?" And he ordered them to be baptized in the name of Jesus Christ (Acts 10:1-5, 38-48a NASU).

This is part of the promise of God through Jeremiah and Ezekiel:

"But this is the covenant which I will make with the house of Israel after those days," declares the Lord, "I will put My law within them and on their heart I will write it; and I will be their God, and they shall be My people" (Jeremiah 31:33 NASU).

And I will give them one heart, and put a new spirit within them. And I will take the heart of stone out of their flesh and give them a heart of flesh (Ezekiel 11:19 NASU).

Requirement for Priesthood

The offering of blood required "a priesthood." Not as in the Levitical priesthood, which was established under the Mosaic Law to give continual sacrificial offerings to God. Jesus Christ only had to offer blood, His blood, once.

Jesus continues His Priesthood forever (Hebrews 7:24) and is, therefore, able to save forever those who draw near to God through Him, since He lives forever to make intercession for them (Hebrews 7:25). He entered the Holy Place in heaven and offered His precious blood once for all, having obtained eternal redemption for all, because without the shedding of blood there is no forgiveness of sins (Hebrews 9:22b).

God has purchased our freedom with his blood and has forgiven all our sins (Colossians 1:14 NLT).

So Christ has now become the High Priest over all the good things that have come. He has entered that great, perfect sanctuary in heaven, not made by human hands and not part of this created world. Once for all time he took blood into that Most Holy Place, but not the blood of goats and calves. He took his own blood, and with it secured our salvation forever (Hebrews 9:11–12 NLT).

For Christ has entered into heaven itself to appear now before God as our Advocate. He did not go into the earthly place of worship, for that was merely a copy of the real Temple in heaven. Nor did he enter heaven to offer himself again and again, like the earthly high priest who enters the Most Holy Place year after year to offer the blood of an animal. If that had been necessary, he would have had to die again and again, ever since the world began. But no! He came once for all time, at the end of the age, to remove the power of sin forever by his sacrificial death for us (Hebrews 9:24–26 NLT).

And so, dear brothers and sisters, we can boldly enter heaven's Most Holy Place because of the blood of Jesus. This is the new, life-giving way that Christ has opened up for us through the sacred curtain, by means of his death for us (Hebrews 10:19–20 NLT).

NECESSITY OF THE REBIRTH

Mankind Prior to Disobedience

God's revelation to mankind through the power of the Holy Spirit (by means of the Holy Scripture) was the way God chose to make Himself known. Mankind was to be made in His image, which according to Jesus is "Spirit" (John 4:24).

Prior to his disobedience, mankind probably could have been translated from life on this earth, according to His will and timing, to a different level of existence (1 Thessalonians 4:15–17), but beginning at the point of disobedience this was no longer generally available to mankind. The notable exceptions are the two men mentioned in the Old Testament: Enoch (Genesis 5:24) and Elijah (2 Kings 2:11).

After the disobedience, man's body returned to the earth but his spirit went to Sheol to await the incarnation and crucifixion and Jesus' visit to paradise. Some believe that those in Sheol could have been given the opportunity to accept or reject Jesus. (1 Peter 3:19–20; 4:6 NASU).

God's Intent Prior to Disobedience

God created mankind to uniquely express Himself. It appears that it was His intent to establish His kingdom on this earth. In order to do this, He created man and woman and empowered them to create more bodies and souls. It is probable that He gave to Adam and Eve *psuche*, natural or human life, but not *Zoe*; the kind of life God gives, known as eternal life. *Psuche* and *Zoe* are two different Greek words commonly translated as life in the English translation of the Bible. *Psuche* commonly refers to natural or human life; whereas, *Zoe* is it the kind of life God gives.

Satan: Initiator of Disobedience

Why did God's creation, Adam and Eve, sin so early and so readily by disobedience?

It probably was because God had not given them Zoe, but was intent on developing their human spirit, psuche, and later to give them Zoe. The initiator of this disobedience was Satan who wanted to destroy God's "image and likeness." This is stated in Scripture:

I will make myself like the Most High (Isaiah 14:14b NASU).

Jesus said in John 10:10 (NASU): "The thief [*Satan*] comes only to steal and kill and destroy." Satan, himself a creation of God (Ezekiel 28:12-15 NASU), has always wanted to destroy or prevent the establishment of God's kingdom on this earth.

Given that God sent Satan to earth because of his disobedience, it was certainly of prime importance to the deceiver that God not be able to set up His kingdom here.

Adam and Eve accepted the counsel of Satan perhaps because of their innocent, trusting and meek nature and the absence of mature, spiritual discernment (absence of Zoe). Their spiritual discernment was in the process of development and Satan, knowing this, beguiled them at its immature stage.

The Trees in the Garden

We know that there were two important trees in the Garden of Eden: the tree of good and evil (Genesis 2:16–17

NASU) and the tree of life (earthly life) spoken of by the LORD God in Genesis 3:22. God said that Adam and Eve could eat from any of the trees in the Garden, except of the tree of the knowledge of good and evil (Genesis 2:16–17).

Evidently, God had plans for granting them eternal (spiritual) life, Zoe, at some stage in their development, but it was thwarted when they ate from the forbidden tree in disobedience. God said that they had, by eating from the tree of good and evil, "become, like one of us" and next they might eat of the tree of life and live forever (Genesis 3:22).

They must have, however, been eating from the tree of life, since God said that they could eat from any of the trees in the garden, which would have included the tree of life. This implied that they had immortal life on this earth. By eating from the tree of good and evil, immortal life on this earth ceased and they could no longer eat from the tree of life.

> Just as through one man [*Adam*] sin entered into the world, and death through sin, and so death spread to all men, because all sinned (Romans 5:12 NASU).

They, therefore, were thrust out of the garden and could no longer partake of the tree of life (Revelation 2:7b).

God's Plan After the Disobedience

After the disobedience, it was going to take time for God to reconstruct His image and likeness: spirit, soul, and body. This was necessary to enable Him to become incarnate in His creation, man.

What was the ultimate goal?

Man's body and soul would be able to house God. His Spirit with Zoe could also dwell and function in man's spirit at the highest level of power. That's why God had to teach man why and how to worship Him and to depend completely upon Him.

God needed a person in whom he could lodge His seed for such a development. He found that person in Abraham: the father of our faith. The end result of Abraham's faith set the world stage for Jesus Christ of Nazareth: the true initiator of God's kingdom on this earth.

God loved his creation even though Adam and Eve's disobedience brought the pollution of sin into the world. He immediately made a way for mankind to return to the Creator. In order to bring about this reconciliation, God the Father chose a people, beginning with Abraham, through whom He'd send a mighty redeemer to the world.

His chosen people were the Israelites and the chosen One was Jesus, the second person of the Trinity: born of a virgin by the power of the Holy Spirit and whose blood also had the imprint of His Father in heaven. Mary's vocal consent and confession (Luke 1:28–38; Romans 9:8) brought the life-giving power of the blood of the Father to mankind. Now it is those who follow Jesus as Savior and Lord that are God's chosen. We know that the blood of the father and mother impacts every child's blood.

> But when the fullness of the time came, God sent forth His Son, born of a woman, born under the Law, so that He might redeem those who were under the Law, that we might receive the adoption as sons (Galatians 4:4–5 NASU).

> Christ Jesus, who, although he existed in the form of God, did not regard equality with God a thing to be

grasped, but emptied Himself, taking the form of a bondservant, {and} being made in the likeness of men. Being found in appearance as a man, He humbled Himself by becoming obedient to the point of death, even the death on a cross (Philippians 2:5b–8 NASU).

Why Did Jesus Die?

God, the Father, had to replace Adam with a new creature, in His image—spirit, soul, body. The old image, man—spirit, soul, and body—had to be destroyed and it was destroyed by Jesus' death on the Cross.

Jesus noted in Mark 12:35–37 that the scribes were saying the Messiah would be a son of David, but Jesus quoted scripture that the Messiah would actually be David's Lord, implying a different kind of lineage—not purely natural. His body came from the seed of Abraham (Matthew 1:1; Luke 3:23–38; 2 Timothy 2:8). The natural spirit (psuche) of the new man, Jesus, came from the seed of Abraham and His blood's origin was, in part from His Father.

The natural spirit of Jesus was given Zoe at his birth (Matthew 1:18; Luke 1:35) and further empowered at His water baptism by John in the Jordan (Matthew 3:16; Acts 10:38) at the same time as His spiritual baptism in the Holy Spirit. This new image—spirit, soul and body—was later raised by the power of the Holy Spirit (Romans 1:2–4 NIV).

The life of His body was impacted by the blood of His Father (Leviticus 17:11) and the life of His Spirit came from his Father. The life of His soul developed as He matured within the family of Mary and Joseph, His siblings and His Temple associates.

Thanks to God we have a Savior who has experienced all of the temptations that we experience and who comes to our aid. With His Resurrection, the spirit, soul, or body of the new man could not suffer eternal death since they were of the Father and therefore linked forever to eternal life.

For we do not have a high priest who cannot sympathize with our weaknesses, but One who has been tempted in all things as {we are, yet} without sin (Hebrews 4:15; see also, Hebrews 2:18 and 1 Peter 2:22 NASU).

Although He was a Son, He learned obedience from the things which He suffered. And having been made perfect, He became to all those who obey Him the source of eternal salvation (Hebrews 5:8–9 NASU).

To repeat: Why was Jesus' death necessary? In order to initiate this new creation, the old man with his natural spirit, soul and body and inheritance from the disobedient Adam had to be put to death. Thus the necessity for the crucifixion of Jesus, who led a perfect life, yet offered His physical body to the Father to take our place on Calvary's Cross.

Shedding the blood of Jesus brought about the physical redemption of God's creation: death of the old man and opening the way to a new creation (Romans 8:11 NASU, NLT).

Our Rebirth

Adam and Eve's disobedience revealed disbelief in God's Word.

In order for mankind to return to His presence as part of His kingdom, rebirth has to take place, beginning with the spirit. This rebirth occurs by man acknowledging the Resurrection of Jesus in his heart (spirit) and confessing with his mouth that Jesus is his Lord and Master. Jesus is, in essence, God incarnate (Colossians 2:9; 1 Timothy 3:16 NASU/NLT).

Mankind is given the opportunity to reverse Adam and Eve's disbelief and disobedience by acknowledging that Jesus is also of the Godhead. He is the Messiah as shown to us by His Resurrection.

By acknowledging in one's heart that God the Father raised Jesus, His Son, from physical and spiritual death, one is giving heart belief to the power of God the Father, Who by the work of the Holy Spirit enables God to return to His original design of establishing His kingdom on this earth.

By confessing with one's mouth that Jesus is Lord, mankind is returning to obedience to the Father, thus reversing the disobedience that initiated this whole process.

With our lives renewed in Christ, we're ready to enter into God's will by obeying the Ten Commandments, following through on Jesus' Sermon on the Mount and acting on the teachings in the New Testament Epistles.

WHAT FOLLOWS REBIRTH

God Indwells Believers

The new eternal spirit, Zoe, is imparted to His chosen by vocal confession that Jesus is their Lord, by belief in their heart that the Father raised Him from the dead, and by belief in what the blood of Jesus did and still does for them. His chosen are empowered by the Baptism of the Holy Spirit and nourished by worshiping Him and by partaking at The Lord's Supper.

Once again, it is important to be reminded that this is not a matter of the intellect or "head" faith or mental assent; it is a matter of heart faith. More specifically, I interpret this to mean an experiential relationship, an "in-the-gut experience" with Jesus.

The seriousness of a relationship to Christ is explained by Jesus in the Parable of the Sower:

> And He said, To you it has been given to know the mysteries of the kingdom of God, but to the rest it is given in parables, that "Seeing they may not see. And hearing they may not understand." Now the parable is this: The seed is the word of God. Those by the wayside are the ones who hear; then the devil comes and takes away the word out of their hearts, lest they should believe and be saved. But the ones on the rock are those who, when they hear, receive the word with joy; and these have no root, who believe for a while and in time of temptation fall away. Now the ones that fell among thorns are those who, when they have heard, go out and are choked with cares, riches, and pleasures of life, and bring no fruit to maturity. But the ones that fell on the good ground are those who, having heard the word with a noble and good heart, keep it and bear fruit with patience (Luke 8:10–15 NKJV).

Indwelling of the Holy Spirit

After a person is spiritually reborn, receiving Zoe (the kind of life God gives), he can receive the indwelling of the Holy Spirit by baptism. Then He is able to function with the gifts and fruits of the Holy Spirit, as Jesus did after his water and spiritual baptisms at the Jordan River (Matthew 3:16; John 1:33; Acts 10:38).

The reason for this empowering, as it was with Jesus, is to enable the believer to "fight the good fight of faith" (1 Timothy 6:12) against Satan and his cohorts.

Satan, the god of this evil world has blinded the minds of those who don't believe, so they are unable to see the glorious light of the Good News that is shining upon them (2 Corinthians 4:4 NLT).

Jesus came to destroy the powers of the devil and to establish his Father's kingdom on this Earth, completing what the Father had begun with Adam and Eve (Colossians 2:15; 1 John 3:8). Jesus promised this empowering:

On the last day, the climax of the festival [*Festival of Shelters*], Jesus stood and shouted to the crowds, "If you are thirsty, come to me! If you believe in me, come and drink! For the scriptures declare that rivers of living water will flow out from within." (When he said 'living water,' he was speaking of the Spirit, who would be given to everyone believing in him. But the Spirit had not yet been given, because Jesus had not yet entered into his glory (John 7:37–39 NLT).

Strength to Resist the Enemy

Man is made up of spirit, soul, and body. As noted above, his spirit can be reborn and have the indwelling of the Father, Son, and Holy Spirit. After this spiritual rebirth (Zoe), he develops and strengthens his spirit (psuche) by receiving the baptism of the Holy Spirit, and by using his spiritual language in prayer and in worship.

He now has a God-given desire to develop and strengthen his soul by reading, confessing, and applying the Scriptures, by using his spiritual language and by participating in the life of a Christian community as well as in his own family. He also has a reason and motivation for bringing his body into subjection to his spirit and offering it as a sacrifice, which the Scriptures describe as worship:

> Therefore I urge you, brethren, by the mercies of God, to present your bodies a living and holy sacrifice, acceptable to God, {which is} your spiritual service of worship (Romans 12:1 NASU).

By worshiping God privately and corporately with fellow believers, the Christian enters into His presence and obtains empowerment for his entire being: spirit, soul, and body.

By partaking at The Lord's Supper, the believer obtains further empowerment to his tripartite being.

Lay the Foundation

By faith (Romans 3:31 NLT), a gift of the grace of God (Ephesians 2:8 NASU), and by the power of the indwelling Holy Spirit, the Christian is able to keep God's commandments, to be true to his confession of Jesus as his Lord and to be obedient (see Part III).

> Loving God means keeping his commandments, and really, that isn't difficult. For every child of God defeats this evil world by trusting Christ to give the victory. And the ones who win this battle against the world are the ones who believe that Jesus is the Son of God (1 John 5:3–5 NLT).

> I [*Paul*] no longer count on my own goodness or my ability to obey God's law, but I trust Christ to save me ... (Philippians 3:9b NLT).

With this empowerment, the Christian can, along with his brothers and sisters, be used by the Holy Spirit to establish the kingdom of God on this earth.

The Holy Spirit, besides empowering believers to remain obedient to the commandments of God, empowers them to proclaim the Gospel with boldness, while loosing them from the wiles of Satan and his cohorts. He empowers them to cast out demons that are oppressing fellow Christians; empowers them to lay hands on the sick, the believer and non-believer and to see miraculous recoveries; and empowers them to express heartfelt spiritual and physical care by good deeds to all mankind, as does the Father.

> For the kingdom of God does not consist in words but in power (1 Corinthians 4:20 NASU).

> And my [*Paul's*] message and my preaching were not in persuasive words of wisdom, but in demonstration of the Spirit and of power, so that your faith would not rest on the wisdom of man, but on the power of God (1 Corinthians 2:4–5 NASU).

The Christian is thus led by and empowered by the Holy Spirit. He listens to what the Spirit tells him to do, but follows only this inward witness as long as it does not contradict what is said about the same matter in the Holy Bible. He is obedient to the Spirit-filled leaders of his church. Otherwise, he may find himself beguiled by the deceiver.

> Beloved, do not believe every spirit, but test the spirits, whether they are of God; because many false prophets have gone out into the world. By this you know the Spirit of God: Every spirit that confesses that Jesus Christ has come in the flesh is of God, and

every spirit that does not confess that Jesus Christ has come in the flesh is not of God. And this is the spirit of the Antichrist, which you have heard was coming, and is now already in the world (1 John 4:1–3 NKJV).

Let us continue in prayer and, if need be, with fasting until the power of the Holy Spirit's fire comes to burn the dross from our spirit. He rids us of all that is not pleasing to the Father. This is the fire that John the Baptist spoke about concerning Jesus when he said that Jesus would baptize with the Spirit and with fire. This is the fire that occurred at Pentecost. Through this fire, God sees His reflection in our spirit, much like when gold is boiled and the dross is skimmed off.

MY NOTES

MY NOTES

MY NOTES

MY NOTES

MY NOTES

My Notes

MY NOTES

Salvation Prayer List

A godly response to learning more about salvation is a greater desire to share the Good News with others. A simple four-point plan is listed below to help you to be highly effective in sharing salvation with family and friends.

Heart of Compassion

Ask God to give you a heart of love and compassion for other people. Think of Jesus and the compassion He has for you and other people. As you develop a heart to see people saved, you'll have more and more opportunities to share what God has done for you.

Prayer Invades the Impossible!

Prayerfully identify the three people you know who are *most likely* to trust Jesus Christ as Savior. For the next thirty days pray for them consistently and frequently. You may want to fast (eating no solid food) once per week as you pray for them to be saved.

Show Warmth and Friendship

In the middle of the thirty days of prayer, invite each person out for coffee or lunch. Have a casual conversation and listen. Build trust by listening and sharing everyday experiences. As he or she talks about things that are happening in his or her life, you'll see certain needs.

Extend an Invitation

At the end of the thirty days, invite your friends to a church service, small group meeting, or casual event where Christians will be together. Look for an opportunity to share what Jesus has done for you.

SALVATION PRAYER LIST

Use the lists below by entering a month and the names of three people. Start a new list each month.

My three *most likely* for _____

1) _____

2) _____

3) _____

Notes:

My three *most likely* for _____

1) _____

2) _____

3) _____

Notes:

My three *most likely* for _____

1) _____

2) _____

3) _____

Notes:

SALVATION PRAYER LIST

Use the lists below by entering a month and the names of three people. Start a new list each month.

My three *most likely* for _____

1) _____

2) _____

3) _____

Notes:

My three *most likely* for _____

1) _____

2) _____

3) _____

Notes:

My three *most likely* for _____

1) _____

2) _____

3) _____

Notes:

SALVATION PRAYER LIST

Use the lists below by entering a month and the names of three people. Start a new list each month.

My three *most likely* for _____

1) _____

2) _____

3) _____

Notes:

My three *most likely* for _____

1) _____

2) _____

3) _____

Notes:

My three *most likely* for _____

1) _____

2) _____

3) _____

Notes:

Salvation Prayer List

Use the lists below by entering a month and the names of three people. Start a new list each month.

My three *most likely* for _____

1) _____

2) _____

3) _____

Notes:

My three *most likely* for _____

1) _____

2) _____

3) _____

Notes:

My three *most likely* for _____

1) _____

2) _____

3) _____

Notes:

PART II

THE
RESURRECTION
GIFT

PART II

THE RESURRECTION GIFT

As for me, I know that my Redeemer lives, And at the last He will take His stand on the earth. Even after my skin is destroyed, yet from my flesh I shall see God; Whom I myself shall behold, And whom my eyes will see and not another. My heart faints within me! (Job 19:25–27 NASU).

Moses said, "THE LORD GOD WILL RAISE UP FOR YOU A PROPHET LIKE ME FROM YOUR BRETHREN; TO HIM YOU SHALL GIVE HEED to everything He says to you. 'And it will be that every soul that does not heed that prophet shall be utterly destroyed from among the people.' And likewise, all the prophets who have spoken, from Samuel and {his} successors onward, also announced these days" (Acts 3:22–24 NASU).

41

God is a Spirit and He speaks to man through man's spirit. Consequently, a belief in God must come through the spirit of man. God can sovereignly make Himself known to man by speaking to man's spirit. God also made it possible for man to know Him by sensual observation of His creation.

The normal way, however, for God to make Jesus known to our spirits is by hearing (reading) and meditating on the Scriptures, which were given to us by the Holy Spirit. Our spirit hears the Word as we read it and we're convicted. Once we believe in our heart (spirit) that what the Scriptures say about Jesus is true—that God raised Him from the dead—our human spirit is reborn to eternal life: it now has Zoe.

With a strong heart belief in the Resurrection of Jesus, I am overcome with power and boldness so that I have a burning desire to tell others. Is this something that I am entitled to as a Christian? Didn't Jesus say to those who believed in Him that they would do greater things than He did? (John 14:12).

How then, can I as a Christian obtain the strong heart belief in the Resurrection of Jesus? It is a gift. I ask for it based on Scripture and then believe that I receive.

WHAT WAS THE RESURRECTION OF JESUS?

The Resurrection of Jesus was the culmination of God's plan to demonstrate His love, His power, and His control. It was the most important and the most powerful event to date for planet Earth. God the Father, through Jesus, regained spiritual dominance of earth through His image and likeness, that is, through His chosen.

From Adam until Christ's Resurrection, God's power to work through His image and likeness was limited, because Adam's spirit and all of mankind's spirit lacked the capacity to be continuously indwelt by the Holy Spirit.

The indwelling made it possible for God to use His chosen for establishing His (spiritual) kingdom on this earth, to provide eternal spiritual life for His chosen and to provide for the physical transformation of His chosen at the first Resurrection.

This power had to be initiated by God Himself since only He has the power to create the outcome. The shedding of Jesus' blood brought forgiveness of the sins of His image and likeness. Jesus' Resurrection offered believers the means of re-entering His spiritual kingdom.

When His chosen accept Jesus as their only and final authority and believe that God the Father raised Jesus from the dead by the power of the Holy Spirit, they become re-created and born-again into His spiritual kingdom.

OTHER BIBLICAL "RESURRECTIONS"

In the Old Testament, the son of the Shunammite woman is raised from the dead by Elisha:

The boy sneezed seven times and opened his eyes (2 Kings 4:35b NIV).

In the New Testament, Jesus raised the son of the widow in the city of Nain (Luke 7:12) and Lazarus (John 11) as well as Jairus's daughter (Mark 5:22–23, 35–43).

Then there are the saints who arose from the dead after Jesus' Resurrection:

> The tombs broke open and the bodies of many holy
> people who had died were raised to life (Matthew
> 27:52 NIV).

How do these differ from the Resurrection of Jesus?

The raising from the dead of the Shunammite woman,
the son of the widow of Naim, Lazarus, Jairus's daughter,
and the saints after Jesus' Resurrection were expressions of
God's love and power for select individuals and groups.
These people all returned to the Earth with no change in
their bodies.

Jesus' Resurrection was with a new, glorified body for a
dramatic change in the existence of mankind in this world.

SIGNIFICANCE OF JESUS' RESURRECTION

To the Cosmos

The Resurrection was opposed by all of the evil powers
of the air and, as noted previously, it brought about a
restructuring of the spiritual forces of the cosmos.

> And Jesus Christ our Lord was shown to be the Son
> of God when God powerfully raised him from the
> dead by means of the Holy Spirit (Romans 1:4
> NLT).

> I pray that you will begin to understand the
> incredible greatness of his power for us who believe
> him. This is the same mighty power that raised
> Christ from the dead and seated him in the place of
> honor at God's right hand in the heavenly realms.
> Now he is far above any ruler or authority or power
> or leader or anything else in this world or in the
> world to come (Ephesians 1:19–21 NLT).

For though we walk in the flesh, we do not war after the flesh: (For the weapons of our warfare are not carnal, but mighty through God to the pulling down of strong-holds;) Casting down imaginations, and every high thing that exalteth itself against the knowledge of God, and bringing into captivity every thought to the obedience of Christ (2 Corinthians 10:3–6 KJV).

For we wrestle not against flesh and blood, but against principalities, against powers, against the rulers of the darkness of this world, against spiritual wickedness in high places (Ephesians 6:12 KJV).

To Spirits in Prison

For Christ also died for sins once for all, {the} just for {the} unjust, so that He might bring us to God, having been put to death in the flesh, but made alive in the spirit; in which also He went and made proclamation to the spirits {now} in prison, who once were disobedient, when the patience of God kept waiting in the days of Noah, during the construction of the ark, in which a few, that is, eight persons, were brought safely through {the} water. Corresponding to that, baptism now saves you—not the removal of dirt from the flesh, but an appeal to God for a good conscience—through the resurrection of Jesus Christ, who is at the right hand of God, having gone into heaven, after angels and authorities and powers had been subjected to Him (1 Peter 3:18–22 NASU).

To His Chosen

For if you confess with your mouth that Jesus is Lord and believe in your heart that God raised him from the dead, you will be saved. For it is by believing in your heart that you are made right with God, and it is by confessing with your mouth that you are saved (Romans 10:9–10 NLT).

For you were buried with Christ when you were baptized. And with him you were raised to a new life because you trusted the mighty power of God, who raised Christ from the dead (Colossians 2:12 NLT).

This is the will of Him who sent Me, that of all that He has given Me I lose nothing, but raise it up on the last day. For this is the will of My Father, that everyone who beholds the Son and believes in Him will have eternal life, and I Myself will raise him up on the last day. ... No one can come to Me unless the Father who sent Me draws him; and I will raise him up on the last day. It is written in the prophets, "AND THEY SHALL ALL BE TAUGHT OF GOD." Everyone who has heard and learned from the Father, comes to Me (John 6:39–40, 44–45 NASU).

In just a little while the world will not see me again, but you will. For I will live again, and you will, too. When I am raised to life again, you will know that I am in my Father, and you are in me, and I am in you (John 14:19–20 NLT).

The Spirit of God, who raised Jesus from the dead, lives in you. And just as he raised Christ from the dead, he will give life to your mortal body by this same Spirit living within you (Romans 8:11 NLT).

For if there is no resurrection of the dead, then Christ has not been raised either. And if Christ was not raised, then all our preaching is useless, and your trust in God is useless. And we apostles would all be lying about God, for we have said that God raised Christ from the grave, but that can't be true if there is no resurrection of the dead. If there is no resurrection of the dead, then Christ has not been raised. And if Christ has not been raised, then your faith is useless, and you are still under condemnation for your sins. In that case, all who have died believing in Christ have perished! And if we have hope in Christ only for this life, we are the most miserable people in the world.

But the fact is that Christ has been raised from the dead. He has become the first of a great harvest of those who will be raised to life again. So you see, just as death came into the world through a man, Adam, now the resurrection from the dead has begun through another man, Christ. Everyone dies because all of us are related to Adam, the first man. But all who are related to Christ, the other man, will be given new life. But there is an order to this resurrection: Christ was raised first; then when Christ comes back, all his people will be raised (1 Corinthians 15:13–23 NLT).

So we are always confident, even though we know that as long as we live in these bodies we are not at home with the Lord. That is why we live by believing and not by seeing. Yes, we are fully confident, and we would rather be away from these bodies, for then we will be at home with the Lord. So our aim is to please him always, whether we are here in this body or away from this body. For we must all stand before Christ to be judged. We will each receive whatever we deserve for the good or evil we have done in our bodies (2 Corinthians 5:6–10 NLT).

For God's way of making us right with himself depends on faith. As a result, I can really know Christ and experience the mighty power that raised him from the dead. I can learn what it means to suffer with him, sharing in his death, so that, somehow, I can experience the resurrection from the dead (Philippians 3:9b–11 NLT).

Blessed be the God and Father of our Lord Jesus Christ, who according to His great mercy has caused us to be born again to a living hope through the resurrection of Jesus Christ from the dead, to {obtain} an inheritance {which is} imperishable and undefiled and will not fade away, reserved in heaven for you, who are protected by the power of God through faith for a salvation ready to be revealed in the last time (1 Peter 1:3–5 NASU).

Through Christ you have come to trust in God. And because God raised Christ from the dead and gave him great glory, your faith and hope can be placed confidently in God. Now you can have sincere love for each other as brothers and sisters because you were cleansed from your sins when you accepted the truth of the Good News. So see to it that you really do love each other intensely with all your hearts. For you have been born again. Your new life did not come from your earthly parents because the life they gave you will end in death. But this new life will last forever because it comes from the eternal, living word of God (1 Peter 1:21–23 NLT).

For if we believe that Jesus died and rose again, even so God will bring with Him those who have fallen asleep in Jesus. For this we say to you by the word of the Lord, that we who are alive and remain until the coming of the Lord, will not precede those who have fallen asleep. For the Lord Himself will descend from heaven with a shout, with the voice of {the} archangel and with the trumpet of God, and the dead in Christ will rise first. Then we who are alive and remain will be caught up together with them in the clouds to meet the Lord in the air, and so we shall always be with the Lord (1 Thessalonians 4:14–17 NASU).

Since you have been raised to new life with Christ, set your sights on the realities of heaven, where Christ sits at God's right hand in the place of honor and power. Let heaven fill your thoughts. Do not think only about things down here on earth. For you died when Christ died, and your real life is hidden with Christ in God. And when Christ, who is your real life, is revealed to the whole world, you will share in all his glory (Colossians 3:1–4 NLT).

But having the same spirit of faith, according to what is written, "I BELIEVED, THEREFORE I SPOKE," we also believe, therefore we also speak, knowing that He who raised the Lord Jesus will raise us also with Jesus and will present us with you (2 Corinthians 4:13–14 NASU).

Then I saw thrones, and they sat on them, and judgment was given to them. And I {saw} the souls of those who had been beheaded because of their testimony of Jesus and because of the word of God, and those who had not worshiped the beast or his image, and had not received the mark on their forehead and on their hand; and they came to life and reigned with Christ for a thousand years. The rest of the dead did not come to life until the thousand years were completed. This is the first resurrection. Blessed and holy is the one who has a part in the first resurrection; over these the second death has no power, but they will be priests of God and of Christ and will reign with Him for a thousand years (Revelation 20:4–6 NASU).

To Planet Earth

Therefore having overlooked the times of ignorance, God is now declaring to men that all {people} everywhere should repent, because He has fixed a day in which He will judge the world in righteousness through a Man whom He has appointed, having furnished proof to all men by raising Him from the dead (Acts 17:30–31 NASU).

For I reckon that the sufferings of this present time are not worthy to be compared with the glory which shall be revealed in us. For the earnest expectation of the creature waiteth for the manifestation of the sons of God. For the creature was made subject to vanity, not willingly, but by reason of him who hath subjected the same in hope, because the creature itself also shall be delivered from the bondage of corruption into the glorious liberty of the children of God. For we know that the whole creation groaneth and travaileth in pain together until now. And not only they, but ourselves also, which have the first fruits of the Spirit, even we ourselves groan within ourselves, waiting for the adoption, to wit, the redemption of our body" (Romans 8:18–23 KJV).

But God is so rich in mercy, and he loved us so very much, that even while we were dead because of our sins, he gave us life when he raised Christ from the dead. (It is only by God's special favor that you have been saved!) For he raised us from the dead along with Christ, and we are seated with him in the heavenly realms—all because we are one with Christ Jesus (Ephesians 2:4–6 NLT).

Afterward He appeared to the eleven themselves as they were reclining {at the table}; and He reproached them for their unbelief and hardness of heart, because they had not believed those who had seen Him after He had risen. And He said to them, "Go into all the world and preach the gospel to all creation. He who has believed and has been baptized shall be saved; but he who has disbelieved shall be condemned. These signs will accompany those who have believed: in My name they will cast out demons, they will speak with new tongues; they will pick up serpents, and if they drink any deadly {poison}, it will not hurt them; they will lay hands on the sick, and they will recover" (Mark 16:14–18 NASU).

For the love of Christ controls us, having concluded this, that one died for all, therefore all died; and He died for all, so that they who live might no longer live for themselves, but for Him who died and rose again on their behalf. Therefore from now on we recognize no one according to the flesh; even though we have known Christ according to the flesh, yet now we know {Him} {in this way} no longer. Therefore if anyone is in Christ, {he is} a new creature; the old things passed away; behold, new things have come (2 Corinthians 5:14–17 NASU).

THE RESURRECTION OF THE DEAD

Jesus said to them, "The sons of this age marry and are given in marriage, but those who are considered worthy to attain to that age and the resurrection from the dead, neither marry nor are given in marriage; for they cannot even die anymore, because they are like angels, and are sons of God, being sons of the resurrection. But that the dead are raised, even Moses showed, in the {passage about the burning} bush, where he calls the Lord THE GOD OF ABRAHAM, AND THE GOD OF ISAAC, AND THE GOD OF JACOB. Now He is not the God of the dead but of the living; for all live to Him (Luke 20:34–38 NASU).

So also is the resurrection of the dead. It is sown a perishable {body}, it is raised an imperishable {body}; it is sown in dishonor, it is raised in glory; it is sown in weakness, it is raised in power; it is sown a natural body, it is raised a spiritual body. If there is a natural body, there is also a spiritual {body}. So also it is written, "The first MAN, ADAM, BECAME A LIVING SOUL." The last Adam {became} a life-giving spirit (1 Corinthians 15:42–45 NASU).

For we know that when this earthly tent we live in is taken down—when we die and leave these bodies—we will have a home in heaven, an eternal body made for us by God himself and not by human hands. We grow weary in our present bodies, and we long for the day when we will put on our heavenly bodies like new clothing. For we will not be spirits without bodies, but we will put on new heavenly bodies. Our dying bodies make us groan and sigh, but it's not that we want to die and have no bodies at all. We want to slip into our new bodies so that these dying bodies will be swallowed up by everlasting life. God himself has prepared us for this, and as a guarantee he has given us his Holy Spirit (2 Corinthians 5:1–5 NLT).

But Thomas, one of the twelve, called Didymus, was not with them when Jesus came. The other disciples therefore said unto him, "We have seen the Lord." But he said unto them, "Except I shall see in his hands the print of the nails, and put my finger into the print of the nails, and thrust my hand into his side, I will not believe." ... And after eight days again his disciples were within, and Thomas with them: then came Jesus, the doors being shut, and stood in the midst, and said, Peace be unto you. Then saith he to Thomas, reach hither thy finger, and behold my hands; and reach hither thy hand, and thrust it into my side: and be not faithless, but believing. And Thomas answered and said unto him, My Lord and my God. Jesus saith unto Him, Thomas, because thou hast seen me, thou hast believed: blessed are they that have not seen, and yet have believed (John 20:24–29 KJV).

MY NOTES

My Notes

MY NOTES

MY NOTES

PART III

LAYING THE FOUNDATION

PART III

LAYING THE FOUNDATION

Now, who will want to harm you if you are eager to do good? But even if you suffer for doing what is right, God will reward you for it. So don't be afraid and don't worry. Instead, you must worship Christ as Lord of your life. And if you are asked about your Christian hope, always be ready to explain it. But you must do this in a gentle and respectful way. Keep your conscience clear. Then if people speak evil against you, they will be ashamed when they see what a good life you live because you belong to Christ. Remember, it is better to suffer for doing good, if that is what God wants, than to suffer for doing wrong (1 Peter 3:13–17 NLT).

In this section, I have presented what I believe the Scriptures are telling us about the basic requirements for laying the foundation of the kingdom of God.

First, each of us must have a focus and that focus must obviously be God. He asks us to worship Him. It is the same request that He made of the Israelites when He had Moses bring them out of Egypt. Pharaoh was to let His people go, so that they could worship Him in the manner He was going to explain to Moses. In the New Testament, His disciples were worshiping Him continuously (Acts 1:12–14; 2:46–47) prior to when the Holy Spirit came upon them and afterwards.

Second, the Scriptures suggest that God has certain requirements for those He has chosen as warriors to lay the foundation of His kingdom:

> And when the king came in to see the guests, he saw there a man which had not on a wedding garment: And he saith unto him, "Friend, how camest thou in hither not having a wedding garment?" And he was speechless. Then said the king to the servants, "Bind him hand and foot, and take him away, and cast him into outer darkness; there shall be weeping and gnashing of teeth. For many are called, but few are chosen" (Matthew 22:11–14 KJV).

Third, since God is a God of order, it is reasonable that we find basic scriptural guidelines, corporate as well as individual, for carrying out the responsibilities that He requires from us.

Fourth, since God is good, He provides scriptural instructions to enable His chosen to become obedient and continue in obedience to His Commandments.

Fifth, the end result is the laying of the foundation of His kingdom for the return of His Son, Our Lord and Savior, Jesus Christ.

Not all of the Scriptures on any of the previous subjects have been cited. There are many more scriptural citations on these topics. I hope this digest will give us, as mentioned in the introduction to the book, a burning desire to pray to the Holy Spirit that He will guide us in further study and enable us to listen when He speaks to us through these Scriptures.

WORSHIP OF GOD

God is Obeyed and Glorified

In the year King Uzziah died, I saw the Lord. He was sitting on a lofty throne, and the train of his robe filled the Temple. Hovering around him were mighty seraphim, each with six wings. With two wings they covered their faces, with two they covered their feet, and with the remaining two they flew. In a great chorus they sang, "Holy, holy, holy is the LORD Almighty! The whole earth is filled with his glory!" The glorious singing shook the Temple to its foundations, and the entire sanctuary was filled with smoke (Isaiah 6:1–4 NLT).

Then as I looked, I saw a door standing open in heaven, and the same voice I had heard before spoke to me with the sound of a mighty trumpet blast. The voice said, "Come up here, and I will show you what must happen after these things." And instantly I was in the Spirit, and I saw a throne in heaven and someone sitting on it! The one sitting on the throne was as brilliant as gemstones—jasper and carnelian.

And the glow of an emerald circled his throne like a rainbow. Twenty-four thrones surrounded him, and twenty-four elders sat on them. They were all clothed in white and had gold crowns on their heads. And from the throne came flashes of lightning and the rumble of thunder. And in front of the throne were seven lampstands with burning flames. They are the seven spirits of God. In front of the throne was a shiny sea of glass, sparkling like crystal. In the center and around the throne were four living beings, each covered with eyes, front and back. The first of these living beings had the form of a lion; the second looked like an ox; the third had a human face; and the fourth had the form of an eagle with wings spread out as though in flight.

Each of these living beings had six wings, and their wings were covered with eyes, inside and out. Day after day and night after night they keep on saying, "Holy, holy, holy is the Lord God Almighty—the one who always was, who is, and who is still to come." Whenever the living beings give glory and honor and thanks to the one sitting on the throne, the one who lives forever and ever, the twenty-four elders fall down and worship the one who lives forever and ever. And they lay their crowns before the throne and say, "You are worthy, O Lord our God, to receive glory and honor and power. For you created everything, and it is for your pleasure that they exist and were created." Revelation 4:1–11 NLT).

God's Chosen Are Cared For

If you fully obey the LORD your God by keeping all the commands I am giving you today, the LORD your God will exalt you above all the nations of the world. You will experience all these blessings if you obey the LORD your God: You will be blessed in your towns and in the country. You will be blessed with many children and productive fields. You will be blessed with fertile herds and flocks. You will be blessed with baskets overflowing with fruit, and with kneading bowls filled with bread. You will be blessed wherever you go, both in coming and in going. The LORD will conquer your enemies when they attack you. They will attack you from one direction, but they will scatter from you in seven. The LORD will bless everything you do and will fill your storehouses with grain. The LORD your God will bless you in the land he is giving you. If you obey the commands of the LORD your God and walk in his ways, the LORD will establish you as his holy people as he solemnly promised to do. Then all the nations of the world will see that you are a people claimed by the LORD, and they will stand in awe of you. The LORD will give you an abundance of good things in the land he swore to give your ancestors—many children, numerous livestock, and abundant crops. The LORD will send rain at the proper time from his rich treasury in the heavens to bless all the work you do. You will lend to many nations, but you will never need to borrow from them. If you listen to these commands of the LORD your God and carefully obey them, the LORD will make you the head and not the tail, and you will always have the upper hand. You must not turn away from any of the commands I am giving you today to follow after other gods and worship them (Deuteronomy 28:1–14 NLT).

Then I saw a new heaven and a new earth, for the old heaven and the old earth had disappeared. And the sea was also gone. And I saw the holy city, the new Jerusalem, coming down from God out of heaven like a beautiful bride prepared for her husband. I heard a loud shout from the throne, saying, "Look, the home of God is now among his people He will live with them, and they will be his people. God himself will be with them. He will remove all of their sorrows, and there will be no more death or sorrow or crying or pain. For the old world and its evils are gone forever." And the one sitting on the throne said, "Look, I am making all things new" And then he said to me, "Write this down, for what I tell you is trustworthy and true." And he also said, "It is finished! I am the Alpha and the Omega—the Beginning and the End. To all who are thirsty I will give the springs of the water of life without charge! All who are victorious will inherit all these blessings, and I will be their God, and they will be my children. But cowards who turn away from me, and unbelievers, and the corrupt, and murderers, and the immoral, and those who practice witchcraft, and idol worshipers, and all liars—their doom is in the lake that burns with fire and sulfur. This is the second death."

No temple could be seen in the city, for the Lord God Almighty and the Lamb are its temple. And the city has no need of sun or moon, for the glory of God illuminates the city, and the Lamb is its light. The nations of the earth will walk in its light, and the rulers of the world will come and bring their glory to it. Its gates never close at the end of day because there is no night. And all the nations will bring their glory and honor into the city. Nothing evil will be allowed to enter—no one who practices shameful idolatry and dishonesty—but only those whose names are written in the Lamb's Book of Life Revelation 21:1–8, 22–27 NLT).

And the angel showed me a pure river with the water of life, clear as crystal, flowing from the throne of God and of the Lamb, coursing down the center of the main street. On each side of the river grew a tree of life, bearing twelve crops of fruit, with a fresh crop each month. The leaves were used for medicine to heal the nations. No longer will anything be cursed. For the throne of God and of the Lamb will be there, and his servants will worship him. And they will see his face, and his name will be written on their foreheads. And there will be no night there—no need for lamps or sun—for the Lord God will shine on them. And they will reign forever and ever.

Then the angel said to me, "These words are trustworthy and true: The Lord God, who tells his prophets what the future holds, has sent his angel to tell you what will happen soon" (Revelation 22:1–6 NLT).

CHOSEN FOR THE KINGDOM

According to Jesus:

Ye have not chosen me, but I have chosen you, and ordained you, that ye should go and bring forth fruit, and that your fruit should remain: that whatsoever ye shall ask of the Father in my name, he may give it you. ... If ye were of the world, the world would love his own: but because ye are not of the world, but I have chosen you out of the world, therefore the world hateth you (John 15:16, 19 KJV).

For many are called, but few are chosen (Matthew 22:14 KJV).

Enter ye in at the strait gate: for wide is the gate, and broad is the way, that leadeth to destruction, and many there be which go in thereat: Because strait is the gate, and narrow is the way, which leadeth unto life, and few there be that find it (Matthew 7:13–14 KJV).

In fact, unless the Lord shortens that time of calamity, the entire human race will be destroyed. But for the sake of his chosen ones he has shortened those days (Mark 13:20 NLT).

For false messiahs and false prophets will rise up and perform miraculous signs and wonders so as to deceive, if possible, even God's chosen ones. Watch out I have warned you (Mark 13:22–23 NLT).

And he will send forth his angels to gather together his chosen ones from all over the world—from the farthest ends of the earth and heaven (Mark 13:27 NLT).

Do not be afraid, little flock, for your Father has chosen gladly to give you the kingdom (Luke 12:32 NASU. See also Deuteronomy 7:7).

According to Peter:

Peter, an apostle of Jesus Christ, to those who reside as aliens, scattered throughout Pontus, Galatia, Cappadocia, Asia, and Bithnia, who are chosen according to the foreknowledge of God the Father, by the sanctifying work of the Spirit, to obey Jesus Christ and be sprinkled with His blood: May grace and peace be yours in the fullest measure (1 Peter 1:1–2 NASU).

And coming to Him as to a living stone which has been rejected by men, but is choice and precious in the sight of God, you also, as living stones, are being built up as a spiritual house for a holy priesthood, to offer up spiritual sacrifices acceptable to God through Jesus Christ (1 Peter 2:4–5 NASU).

According to Paul:

According as he hath chosen us in him before the foundation of the world, that we should be holy and without blame before him in love: Having predestinated us unto the adoption of children by Jesus Christ to himself, according to the good pleasure of his will, to the praise of the glory of his grace, wherein he hath made us accepted in the beloved (Ephesians 1:4–6 KJV).

And we know that God causes everything to work together for the good of those who love God and are called according to his purpose for them (Romans 8:28).

And having chosen them, he called them to come to him. And he gave them right standing with himself, and he promised them his glory. ... Who dares accuse us whom God has chosen for his own? Will God? No! He is the one who has given us right standing with himself (Romans 8:30, 33 NLT).

But if our gospel be hid, it is hid to them that are lost: In whom the god of this world hath blinded the minds of them which believe not, lest the light of the glorious gospel of Christ, who is the image of God, should shine unto them. For we preach not ourselves, but Christ Jesus the Lord; and ourselves your servants for Jesus' sake. For God, who commanded the light to shine out of darkness, hath shined in our hearts, to give the light of the knowledge of the glory of God in the face of Jesus Christ. But we have this treasure in earthen vessels, that the excellency of the power may be of God, and not of us (2 Corinthians 4:3–7 KJV).

So, as those who have been chosen of God, holy and beloved, put on a heart of compassion, kindness, humility, gentleness and patience (Colossians 3:12 NASU).

I [*Paul*] have been sent to bring faith to those God has chosen and to teach them to know the truth that shows them how to live godly lives (Titus 1:1b. NLT).

But we should always give thanks to God for you, brethren beloved of the Lord, because God has chosen you from the beginning for salvation through sanctification by the Spirit and faith in the truth (2 Thessalonians 2:13 NASU).

As Mentioned by the Angel:

These shall make war with the Lamb, and the Lamb shall overcome them: for he is Lord of lords, and King of kings: and they that are with him are called, and chosen, and faithful (Revelation 17:14 KJV).

Requirements for Chosen Warriors

Spiritual Rebirth

Even in his own land and among his own people, he was not accepted. But to all who believed him and accepted him, he gave the right to become children of God. They are reborn! This is not a physical birth resulting from human passion or plan—this rebirth comes from God (John 1:11–13 NLT).

Jesus replied, "I assure you, unless you are born again, you can never see the Kingdom of God." "What do you mean?" exclaimed Nicodemus. "How can an old man go back into his mother's womb and be born again?" Jesus replied, "The truth is, no one can enter the Kingdom of God without being born of water and the Spirit. Humans can reproduce only human life, but the Holy Spirit gives new life from heaven. So don't be surprised at my statement that you must be born again. Just as you can hear the wind but can't tell where it comes from or where it is going, so you can't explain how people are born of the Spirit" (John 3:3–8 NLT).

For if you confess with your mouth that Jesus is Lord and believe in your heart that God raised him from the dead, you will be saved. For it is by believing in your heart that you are made right with God, and it is by confessing with your mouth that you are saved (Romans 10:9–10 NLT).

For you have been born again. Your new life did not come from your earthly parents because the life they gave you will end in death. But this new life will last forever because it comes from the eternal, living word of God (1 Peter 1:23 NLT).

Whoever confesses that Jesus is the Son of God, God abides in him, and he in God (1 John 4:15 NKJV).

Water Baptism

So let it be clearly known by everyone in Israel that God has made this Jesus whom you crucified to be both Lord and Messiah!

Peter's words convicted them deeply, and they said to him and to the other apostles, "Brothers, what should we do?" Peter replied, "Each of you must turn from your sins and turn to God, and be baptized in the name of Jesus Christ for the forgiveness of your sins. Then you will receive the gift of the Holy Spirit. This promise is to you and to your children, and even to the Gentiles—all who have been called by the Lord our God" (Acts 2:36–39 NLT).

Or have you forgotten that when we became Christians and were baptized to become one with Christ Jesus, we died with him? For we died and were buried with Christ by baptism. And just as Christ was raised from the dead by the glorious power of the Father, now we also may live new lives. Since we have been united with him in his death, we will also be raised as he was. Our old sinful selves were crucified with Christ so that sin might lose its power in our lives. We are no longer slaves to sin. For when we died with Christ we were set free from the power of sin. And since we died with Christ, we know we will also share his new life. We are sure of this because Christ rose from the dead, and he will never die again. Death no longer has any power over him (Romans 6:3–9 NLT).

And all who have been united with Christ in baptism have been made like him (Galatians 3:27 NLT).

For you were buried with Christ when you were baptized. And with him you were raised to a new life because you trusted the mighty power of God, who raised Christ from the dead (Colossians 2:12 NLT).

And this is a picture of baptism, which now saves you by the power of Jesus Christ's resurrection. Baptism is not a removal of dirt from your body; it is an appeal to God from a clean conscience (1 Peter 3:21 NLT).

Baptism in the Holy Spirit

I [*John the Baptist*] baptize with water those who turn from their sins and turn to God. But someone is coming soon who is far greater than I am—so much greater that I am not even worthy to be his slave. He will baptize you with the Holy Spirit and with fire (Matthew 3:11 NLT).

I [*John the Baptist*] didn't know he was the one, but when God sent me to baptize with water, he told me, "When you see the Holy Spirit descending and resting upon someone, he is the one you are looking for. He is the one who baptizes with the Holy Spirit." (John 1:33 NLT).

On the last day, the climax of the festival, Jesus stood and shouted to the crowds, "If you are thirsty, come to me! If you believe in me, come and drink!

For the Scriptures declare that rivers of living water will flow out from within." When he said "living water," he was speaking of the Spirit, who would be given to everyone believing in him. But the Spirit had not yet been given, because Jesus had not yet entered into his glory (John 7:37–39 NLT).

In one of these meetings as he was eating a meal with them, he told them, "Do not leave Jerusalem until the Father sends you what he promised. Remember, I have told you about this before. John baptized with water, but in just a few days you will be baptized with the Holy Spirit" (Acts 1:4–5 NLT).

And everyone present was filled with the Holy Spirit and began speaking in other languages, as the Holy Spirit gave them this ability (Acts 2:4 NLT).

The Jewish believers who came with Peter were amazed that the gift of the Holy Spirit had been poured out upon the Gentiles, too. And there could be no doubt about it, for they heard them speaking in tongues and praising God (Acts 10:45–46 NLT).

Then when Paul laid his hands on them, the Holy Spirit came on them, and they spoke in other tongues and prophesied (Acts 19:6 NLT).

I [Paul] wish you all had the gift of speaking in tongues, but even more I wish you were all able to prophesy. For prophecy is a greater and more useful gift than speaking in tongues, unless someone interprets what you are saying so that the whole church can get some good out of it (1 Corinthians 14:5 NLT).

I thank God that I speak in tongues more than all of you (1 Corinthians 14:18 NLT).

So, dear brothers and sisters, be eager to prophesy, and don't forbid speaking in tongues (1 Corinthians 14:39 NLT).

But you, beloved, building yourselves up on your most holy faith, praying in the Holy Spirit (Jude 20 NASU).

Do not quench the Spirit; do not despise prophetic utterances [*gifts*] (1 Thessalonians 5:19–20 NASU).

Now there are diversities of gifts, but the same Spirit. And there are differences of administrations, but the same Lord. And there are diversities of operations, but it is the same God which worketh all in all. But the manifestations of the Spirit are given to every man to profit withal. For to one is given by the Spirit the word of wisdom; to another the word of knowledge by the same Spirit; to another faith by the same Spirit; to another the gifts of healing by the same Spirit. To another the working of miracles; to another prophecy; to another discerning of spirits; to another divers kinds of tongues; to another the interpretation of tongues: But all these worketh that one and the selfsame Spirit, dividing to every man severally as he will (1 Corinthians 12:4–11 KJV).

RESPONSIBILITIES

Corporate Leadership

He [*Christ*] is the one who gave these gifts to the church: the apostles, the prophets, the evangelists, and the pastors and teachers. Their responsibility is to equip God's people to do his work and build up the church, the body of Christ, until we come to such unity in our faith and knowledge of God's Son that we will be mature and full grown in the Lord, measuring up to the full stature of Christ. Then we will no longer be like children, forever changing our minds about what we believe because someone has told us something different or because someone has cleverly lied to us and made the lie sound like the truth. Instead, we will hold to the truth in love, becoming more and more in every way like Christ, who is the head of his body, the church. Under his direction, the whole body is fitted together perfectly. As each part does its own special work, it helps the other parts grow, so that the whole body is healthy and growing and full of love (Ephesians 4:11–16).

It is a true saying that if someone wants to be an elder, he desires an honorable responsibility. For an elder must be a man whose life cannot be spoken against. He must be faithful to his wife. He must exhibit self-control, live wisely, and have a good reputation. He must enjoy having guests in his home and must be able to teach. He must not be a heavy drinker or be violent. He must be gentle, peace loving, and not one who loves money (1 Timothy 3:1–3 NLT).

He [elder] must have a strong and steadfast belief in the trustworthy message he was taught; then he will be able to encourage others with right teaching and show those who oppose it where they are wrong (Titus 1:9 NLT).

I warn and counsel the elders among you (the pastors and spiritual guides of the church) as fellow elder and as an eyewitness [called to testify] of the sufferings of Christ, as well as a sharer in the glory (the honor and splendor) that is to be revealed (disclosed, unfolded): Tend (nurture, guard, guide, and fold) the flock of God that is [your responsibility], not by coercion or constraint, but willingly; not dishonorably motivated by the advantages and profits [belonging to the office], but eagerly and cheerfully; Not domineering [as arrogant, dictatorial, and overbearing persons] over those in your charge, but being examples (patterns and models of Christian living) to the flock (the congregation). And then when the Chief Shepherd is revealed, you will win the conqueror's crown of glory (1 Peter 5:1–4 AMP).

Until I [*Paul*] come, devote yourself to the public reading of Scripture, to preaching and to teaching (1 Timothy 4:13 NIV).

Corporate Worship

He [*Jesus*] taught them, "The Scriptures declare, 'My Temple will be called a place of prayer for all nations'" (Mark 11:17a NLT).

For God is Spirit, so those who worship him must worship in spirit and in truth (John 4:24 NLT).

Praise the LORD! Praise God in his heavenly dwelling; praise him in his mighty heaven! Praise him for his mighty works; praise his unequaled greatness! Praise him with a blast of the trumpet; praise him with the lyre and harp! Praise him with the tambourine and dancing; praise him with stringed instruments and flutes! Praise him with a clash of cymbals; praise him with loud clanging cymbals. Let everything that lives sing praises to the LORD! Praise the LORD! (Psalm 150 NLT).

Make a joyful noise unto the Lord, all ye lands. Serve the Lord with gladness: come before his presence with singing. Know ye that the Lord he is God: it is he that hath made us and not we ourselves; we are his people, and the sheep of his pasture. Enter into his gates with thanksgiving and into his courts with praise: be thankful unto him, and bless his name. For the Lord is good; his mercy is everlasting; and his truth endureth to all generations (Psalm 100 KJV).

Since we are receiving a Kingdom that cannot be destroyed, let us be thankful and please God by worshiping him with holy fear and awe. For our God is a consuming fire (Hebrews 12:28–29 NLT).

They worshiped together at the Temple each day, met in homes for the Lord's Supper, and shared their meals with great joy and generosity—all the while praising God and enjoying the goodwill of all the people. And each day the Lord added to their group those who were being saved (Acts 2:46–47 NLT).

Well, my brothers and sisters, let's summarize what I am saying. When you meet, one will sing, another will teach, another will tell some special revelation God has given, one will speak in an unknown language, while another will interpret what is said. But everything that is done must be useful to all and build them up in the Lord. No more than two or three should speak in an unknown language. They must speak one at a time, and someone must be ready to interpret what they are saying. But if no one is present who can interpret, they must be silent in your church meeting and speak in tongues to God privately. Let two or three prophesy, and let the others evaluate what is said. But if someone is prophesying and another person receives a revelation from the Lord, the one who is speaking must stop. In this way, all who prophesy will have a turn to speak, one after the other, so that everyone will learn and be encouraged. Remember that people who prophesy are in control of their spirit and can wait their turn. For God is not a God of disorder but of peace, as in all the other churches (1 Corinthians 14:26–33 NLT).

But be sure that everything is done properly and in order (1 Corinthians 14:40 NLT).

Corporate Prayer

Then He said to His disciples, "The harvest is plentiful, but the workers are few. Therefore beseech the Lord of the harvest to send out workers into His harvest" (Matthew 9:37–38 NASU).

First of all, then, I urge that entreaties {and} prayers, petitions {and} thanksgivings, be made on behalf of all men, for kings and all who are in authority, so that we may lead a tranquil and quiet life in all godliness and dignity. This is good and acceptable in the sight of God our Savior, who desires all men to be saved and to come to the knowledge of the truth. For there is one God, {and} one mediator also between God and men, {the} man Christ Jesus, who gave Himself as a ransom for all, the testimony {given} at the proper time. For this I was appointed a preacher and an apostle (I am telling the truth, I am not lying) as a teacher of the Gentiles in faith and truth. Therefore I want the men in every place to pray, lifting up holy hands, without wrath and dissension (1 Timothy 2:1–8 NASU).

When they [*Peter and John*] had been released, they went to their own {companions} and reported all that the chief priests and the elders had said to them. And when they heard {this}, they lifted their voices to God with one accord and said, "O Lord, it is You who MADE THE HEAVEN AND THE EARTH AND THE SEA, AND ALL THAT IS IN THEM, who by the Holy Spirit, {through} the mouth of our father David Your servant, said, 'WHY DID THE GENTILES RAGE, AND THE PEOPLES DEVISE FUTILE THINGS? THE KINGS OF THE EARTH TOOK THEIR STAND, AND THE RULERS WERE GATHERED TOGETHER AGAINST THE LORD AND AGAINST HIS CHRIST.

For truly in this city there were gathered together against Your holy servant Jesus, whom You anointed, both Herod and Pontius Pilate, along with the Gentiles and the peoples of Israel, to do whatever Your hand and Your purpose predestined to occur.

And now, Lord, take note of their threats, and grant that Your bond-servants may speak Your word with all confidence, while You extend Your hand to heal, and signs and wonders take place through the name of Your holy servant Jesus."And when they prayed, the place where they had gathered together was shaken, and they were all filled with the Holy

Spirit and {began} to speak the word of God with boldness (Acts 4:23–31 NASU).

Is anyone among you sick? {Then} he must call for the elders of the church and they are to pray over him, anointing him with oil in the name of the Lord; and the prayer offered in faith will restore the one who is sick, and the Lord will raise him up, and if he has committed sins, they will be forgiven him. Therefore, confess your sins to one another so that you may be healed. The effective prayer of a righteous man can accomplish much (James 5:14–16 NASU).

INDIVIDUAL RESPONSIBILITIES

Worship and Prayer

One day soon afterward Jesus went to a mountain to pray, and he prayed to God all night (Luke 6:12 NLT).

About eight days later Jesus took Peter, James, and John to a mountain to pray (Luke 9:28 NLT).

One day Jesus told his disciples a story to illustrate their need for constant prayer and to show them that they must never give up (Luke 18:1 NLT).

Keep on asking, and you will be given what you ask for. Keep on looking, and you will find. Keep on knocking, and the door will be opened. For everyone who asks, receives. Everyone who seeks God finds Him. And the door is opened to everyone who knocks (Matthew 7:7–8 NLT).

Pray without ceasing. In every thing give thanks: for this is the will of God in Christ Jesus concerning you (1 Thessalonians 5:17–18 KJV).

And now about prayer. When you pray, don't be like the hypocrites who love to pray publicly on street corners and in the synagogues where everyone can see them. I assure you, that is all the reward they will ever get. But when you pray, go away by yourself, shut the door behind you, and pray to your Father secretly. Then your Father, who knows all secrets, will reward you. When you pray, don't babble on and on as people of other religions do. They think their prayers are answered only by repeating their words again and again. Don't be like them, because your Father knows exactly what you need even before you ask him!

Pray like this: Our Father in heaven, may your name be honored. May your Kingdom come soon. May your will be done here on earth, just as it is in heaven. Give us our food for today, and forgive us our sins, just as we have forgiven those who have sinned against us. And don't let us yield to temptation, but deliver us from the evil one. If you forgive those who sin against you, your heavenly Father will forgive you. But if you refuse to forgive others, your Father will not forgive your sins (Matthew 6:5–15 NLT).

Tithe of Money

But how terrible it will be for you Pharisees! For you are careful to tithe even the tiniest part of your income, but you completely forget about justice and the love of God. You should tithe, yes, but you should not leave undone the more important things (Luke 11:42 NLT).

For this Melchizedek, king of Salem, priest of the Most High God, who met Abraham as he was returning from the slaughter of the kings and blessed him, to whom also Abraham apportioned a tenth part of all {the spoils}, was first of all, by the translation {of his name}, king of righteousness, and then also king of Salem, which is king of peace. Without father, without mother, without genealogy, having neither beginning of days nor end of life, but made like the Son of God, he remains a priest perpetually. Now observe how great this man was to whom Abraham, the patriarch, gave a tenth of the choicest spoils. And those indeed of the sons of Levi who receive the priest's office have commandment in the Law to collect a tenth from the people, that is, from their brethren, although these are descended from Abraham. But the one whose genealogy is not traced from them collected a tenth from Abraham and blessed the one who had the promises. But without any dispute the lesser is blessed by the greater. In this case mortal men receive tithes, but in that case one {receives them,} of whom it is witnessed that he lives on. And, so to speak, through Abraham even Levi, who received tithes, paid tithes, for he was still in the loins of his father when Melchizedek met him (Hebrews 7:1–10 NASU).

Will a man rob God? Yet you are robbing Me! But you say, "How have we robbed You?" "In tithes and offerings. You are cursed with a curse, for you are robbing Me, the whole nation {of you!} Bring the whole tithe into the storehouse, so that there may be food in My house, and test Me now in this," says the LORD of hosts, "if I will not open for you the windows of heaven and pour out for you a blessing until it overflows. Then I will rebuke the devourer for you, so that it will not destroy the fruits of the ground; nor will your vine in the field cast {its grapes,}" says the LORD of hosts. "All the nations will call you blessed, for you shall be a delightful land," says the LORD of hosts (Malachi 3:8–12 NASU).

Obedience

To what do the chosen have to be obedient to in this world?

One of them, a lawyer, asked Him a question, testing Him, "Teacher, which is the great commandment in the Law?" And He said to him, "YOU SHALL LOVE THE LORD YOUR GOD WITH ALL YOUR HEART, AND WITH ALL YOUR SOUL, AND WITH ALL YOUR MIND. This is the great and foremost commandment. The second is like it, YOU SHALL LOVE YOUR NEIGHBOR AS YOURSELF. On these two commandments depend the whole Law and the Prophets" (Matthew 22:35–40 NASU).

Then God spoke all these words, saying, "I am the LORD your God, who brought you out of the land of Egypt, out of the house of slavery. You shall have no other gods before Me. You shall not make for yourself an idol, or any likeness of what is in heaven above or on the earth beneath or in the water under the earth. You shall not worship them or serve them; for I, the LORD your God, am a jealous God, visiting the iniquity of the fathers on the children, on the third and the fourth generations of those who hate Me, but showing loving kindness to thousands, to those who love Me and keep My commandments. You shall not take the name of the LORD your God in vain, for the LORD will not leave him unpunished who takes His name in vain. Remember the sabbath day, to keep it holy. Six days you shall labor and do all your work, but the seventh day is a sabbath of the LORD your God; {in it} you shall not do any work, you or your son or your daughter, your male or your female servant or your cattle or your sojourner who stays with you. For in six days the LORD made the heavens and the earth, the sea and all that is in them, and rested on the seventh day; therefore the LORD blessed the sabbath day and made it holy.

Honor your father and your mother, that your days may be prolonged in the land which the LORD your God gives you. You shall not murder. You shall not commit adultery. You shall not steal. You shall not bear false witness against your neighbor. You shall not covet your neighbor's house; you shall not covet your neighbor's wife or his male servant or his female servant or his ox or his donkey or anything that belongs to your neighbor" (Exodus 20:1–17 NASU).

Owe nothing to anyone except to love one another; for he who loves his neighbor has fulfilled {the} law (Romans 13:8 NASU).

Don't misunderstand why I have come. I did not come to abolish the Law of Moses or the writings of the prophets. No, I came to fulfill them. I assure you, until heaven and earth disappear, even the smallest detail of God's law will remain until its purpose is achieved (Matthew 5:17–18 NLT).

Well then, if we emphasize faith, does this mean that we can forget about the law? Of course not In fact, only when we have faith do we truly fulfill the law (Romans 3:31 NLT).

His Chosen Become Obedient

Forgiveness

For if you forgive others for their transgressions, your heavenly Father will also forgive you. But if you do not forgive others, then your Father will not forgive your transgressions (Matthew 6:14–15 NASU).

Then Peter came and said to Him, "Lord, how often shall my brother sin against me and I forgive him? Up to seven times?" Jesus said to him, "I do not say to you, up to seven times, but up to seventy times seven" (Matthew 18:21–22 NASU).

Worship

The people whom I have formed for Myself Will declare my praise (Isaiah 43:21 NASU).

Jesus answered him, "It is written, 'YOU SHALL WORSHIP THE LORD YOUR GOD AND SERVE HIM ONLY'" (Luke 4:8 NASU).

For we are the {true} circumcision, who worship the Spirit of God and glory in Christ Jesus and put no confidence in the flesh (Philippians 3:3 NASU).

Reading the Bible

> This book of the law shall not depart from your mouth, but you shall meditate on it day and night, so that you may be careful to do according to all that is written in it; for then you will make your way prosperous, and then you will have success (Joshua 1:8 NASU).

> My son, give attention to my words; Incline your ear to my sayings. Do not let them depart from your sight; Keep them in the midst of your heart. For they are life to those who find them And health to all their body (Proverbs. 4:20–22 NASU).

> All Scripture is inspired by God and profitable for teaching, for reproof, for correction, for training in righteousness; so that the man of God may be adequate, equipped for every good work (2 Timothy 3:16–17 NASU).

> As your words are taught, they give light; even the simple can understand them (Psalm 119:130 NLT).

> So faith {comes} from hearing, and hearing by the word of Christ (Romans 10:17 NASU).

The Lord's Supper

> So Jesus said again, "I assure you, unless you eat the flesh of the Son of Man and drink his blood, you cannot have eternal life within you. But those who eat my flesh and drink my blood have eternal life, and I will raise them at the last day. For my flesh is the true food, and my blood is the true drink. All who eat my flesh and drink my blood remain in me, and I in them. I live by the power of the living

Father who sent me; in the same way, those who partake of me will live because of me. I am the true bread from heaven. Anyone who eats this bread will live forever and not die as your ancestors did, even though they ate the manna" (John 6:53–58 NLT).

Is not the cup of blessing that we bless a sharing in the blood of Christ? Is not the bread that we break a sharing in the body of Christ? Since there is one bread, we who are many are one body; for we all partake of the one bread. ...

For I received from the Lord that which I also delivered to you, that the Lord Jesus in the night in which He was betrayed took bread; and when He had given thanks, He broke it and said, "This is My body, which is for you; do this in remembrance of Me." In the same way {He took} the cup also after supper, saying, "This cup is the new covenant in My blood; do this, as often as you drink {it}, in remembrance of Me." For as often as you eat this bread and drink the cup, you proclaim the Lord's death until He comes. Therefore whoever eats the bread or drinks the cup of the Lord in an unworthy manner, shall be guilty of the body and the blood of the Lord. But a man must examine himself, and in so doing he is to eat of the bread and drink of the cup. For he who eats and drinks, eats and drinks judgment to himself if he does not judge the body rightly. For this reason many among you are weak and sick, and a number sleep. But if we judged ourselves rightly, we would not be judged. But when we are judged, we are disciplined by the Lord so that we will not be condemned along with the world (1 Corinthians 10:16–17; 11:23–32 NASU).

Crucifying the Body

Therefore I urge you, brethren, by the mercies of God, to present your bodies a living and holy sacrifice, acceptable to God, {which is} your spiritual service of worship. And do not be conformed to this world, but be transformed by the renewing of your mind, so that you may prove what the will of God is, that which is good and acceptable and perfect (Romans 12:1–2 NASU).

I have been crucified with Christ; and it is no longer I who live, but Christ lives in me; and the {life} which I now live in the flesh I live by faith in the Son of God, who loved me and gave Himself up for me (Galatians 2:20 NASU).

But put on the Lord Jesus Christ, and make no provision for the flesh in regard to {its} lusts (Romans 13:14 NASU).

For, ALL FLESH IS LIKE GRASS, AND ALL ITS GLORY LIKE THE FLOWER OF GRASS. THE GRASS WITHERS, AND THE FLOWER FALLS OFF (1 Peter 1:24 NASU).

Therefore, since Christ has suffered in the flesh, arm yourselves also with the same purpose, because he who has suffered in the flesh has ceased from sin, so as to live the rest of the time in the flesh no longer for the lusts of men, but for the will of God (1 Peter 4:1–2 NASU).

Therefore do not let sin reign in your mortal body so that you obey its lusts, and do not go on presenting the members of your body to sin {as} instruments of unrighteousness; but present yourselves to God as those alive from the dead, and your members {as} instruments of righteousness to God. For sin shall not be master over you, for you are not under law but under grace (Romans 6:12–14 NASU).

Applying Scriptures

Thou hast magnified thy word above all thy name (Psalm 138:2b KJV).

And He [*Jesus*] is the radiance of His [*God's*] glory and the exact representation of His [*God's*] nature, and upholds all things by the word of His [*Jesus'*] power (Hebrews 1:3a NASU).

Your word is a lamp to my feet And a light to my path (Psalm 119:105 NKJV).

And Jesus answering saith unto them, "Have faith in God. For verily I say unto you, That whosoever shall say unto this mountain, 'Be thou removed, and be thou cast into the sea;' and shall not doubt in his heart, but shall believe that those things which he saith shall come to pass; he shall have whatsoever he saith. Therefore I say unto you, What things soever ye desire, when ye pray, believe that ye receive them, and ye shall have them. And when ye stand praying, forgive, if ye have ought against any: that your Father also which is in heaven may forgive you your trespasses. But if ye do not forgive, neither will your Father which is in heaven forgive your trespasses" (Mark 11:22–26 KJV).

The Name of Jesus

I tell you the truth, anyone who has faith in me will do what I have been doing. He will do even greater things than these, because I am going to the Father. And I will do whatever you ask in my name, so that the Son may bring glory to the Father. You may ask me for anything in my name, and I will do it (John 14:12–14 NIV).

These signs will accompany those who have believed: in My name they will cast out demons (Mark 16:17a NASU).

For this reason also, God highly exalted Him, and bestowed on Him the name which is above every name, so that at the name of Jesus EVERY KNEE WILL BOW, of those who are in heaven and on earth and under the earth (Philippians 2:9–10 NASU).

The name of the LORD is a strong tower; the righteous run to it and are safe (Proverbs 18:10 NKJV).

Not to Worry

For this reason I say to you, do not be worried about your life, {as to} what you will eat or what you will drink; nor for your body, {as to} what you will put on (Matthew 6:25a NASU).

Be anxious for nothing, but in everything by prayer and supplication with thanksgiving let your requests be made known to God. And the peace of God, which surpasses all comprehension, will guard your hearts and your minds in Christ Jesus (Philippians 4:6–7 NASU).

If we confess our sins, He is faithful and righteous to forgive us our sins and to cleanse us from all unrighteousness (1 John 1:9 NASU).

Angelic Assistance

Are they not all ministering spirits, sent out to render service for the sake of those who will inherit salvation? (Hebrews 1:14 NASU).

For He will give His angels [especial] charge over you to accompany and defend and preserve you in all your ways [of obedience and service]. They shall bear you up on their hands, lest you dash your foot against a stone (Psalm 91:11–12 AMP).

Spiritual Support and Growth

Think of ways to encourage one another to outbursts of love and good deeds. And let us not neglect our meeting together, as some people do, but encourage and warn each other, especially now that the day of his coming back again is drawing near (Hebrews 10:24–25 NLT).

Confess your sins to each other and pray for each other so that you may be healed. The earnest prayer of a righteous person has great power and wonderful results (James 5:16 NLT).

JOINT RESPONSIBILILTIES

Ministering to the Chosen

But when the Son of Man comes in His glory, and all the angels with Him, then He will sit on His glorious throne. All the nations will be gathered before Him; and He will separate them from one another, as the shepherd separates the sheep from the goats; and He will put the sheep on His right, and the goats on the left.

Then the King will say to those on His right, 'Come, you who are blessed of My Father, inherit the kingdom prepared for you from the foundation of the world. For I was hungry, and you gave Me {something} to eat; I was thirsty, and you gave Me {something} to drink; I was a stranger, and you invited Me in; naked, and you clothed Me; I was sick, and you visited Me; I was in prison, and you came to Me.' Then the righteous will answer Him, 'Lord, when did we see You hungry, and feed You, or thirsty, and give You {something} to drink? And when did we see You a stranger, and invite You in, or naked, and clothe You? When did we see You sick, or in prison, and come to You?' The King will answer and say to them, 'Truly I say to you, to the extent that you did it to one of these brothers of Mine, {even} the least {of them}, you did it to Me.' Then He will also say to those on His left, 'Depart from Me, accursed ones, into the eternal fire which has been prepared for the devil and his angels; for I was hungry, and you gave Me {nothing} to eat; I was thirsty, and you gave Me nothing to drink; I was a stranger, and you did not invite Me in; naked, and you did not clothe Me; sick, and in prison, and you did not visit Me.' Then they themselves also will answer, 'Lord, when did we see You hungry, or thirsty, or a stranger, or naked, or sick, or in prison, and did not take care of You?' Then He will answer them, 'Truly I say to you, to the extent that you did not do it to one of the least of these, you did not do it to me' (Matthew 25:31–45 NASU).

And if anyone gives even a cup of cold water to one of these little ones because he is my disciple, I tell you the truth, he will certainly not lose his reward (Matthew 10:42 NIV).

If anyone says, "I am living in the light," but hates a Christian brother or sister, that person is still living in darkness. Anyone who loves other Christians is living in the light and does not cause anyone to stumble. Anyone who hates a Christian brother or sister is living and walking in darkness. Such a person is lost, having been blinded by the darkness (1 John 2:9–11 NLT).

This is the message we have heard from the beginning: We should love one another. We must not be like Cain, who belonged to the evil one and killed his brother. And why did he kill him? Because Cain had been doing what was evil, and his brother had been doing what was right. So don't be surprised, dear brothers and sisters, if the world hates you. If we love our Christian brothers and sisters, it proves that we have passed from death to eternal life. But a person who has no love is still dead. Anyone who hates another Christian is really a murderer at heart. And you know that murderers don't have eternal life within them. We know what real love is because Christ gave up his life for us. And so we also ought to give up our lives for our Christian brothers and sisters. But if anyone has enough money to live well and sees a brother or sister in need and refuses to help—how can God's love be in that person? Dear children, let us stop just saying we love each other; let us really show it by our actions. It is by our actions that we know we are living in the truth, so we will be confident when we stand before the Lord, even if our hearts condemn us. For God is greater than our hearts, and he knows everything (1 John 3:11–20 NLT).

Ministering to the World

And a lawyer stood up and put Him to the test, saying, "Teacher, what shall I do to inherit eternal life?" And He said to him, "What is written in the Law? How does it read to you?" And he answered, "YOU SHALL LOVE THE LORD YOUR GOD WITH ALL YOUR HEART, AND WITH ALL YOUR SOUL, AND WITH ALL YOUR STRENGTH, AND WITH ALL YOUR MIND; AND YOUR NEIGHBOR AS YOURSELF." And He said to him, "You have answered correctly; DO THIS AND YOU WILL LIVE." But wishing to justify himself, he said to Jesus, "And who is my neighbor?" Jesus replied and said, "A man was going down from Jerusalem to Jericho, and fell among robbers, and they stripped him and beat him, and went away leaving him half dead. And by chance a priest was going down on that road, and when he saw him, he passed by on the other side. Likewise a Levite also, when he came to the place and saw him, passed by on the other side. But a Samaritan, who was on a journey, came upon him; and when he saw him, he felt compassion, and came to him and bandaged up his wounds, pouring oil and wine on them; and he put him on his own beast, and brought him to an inn and took care of him. On the next day he took out two denarii and gave them to the innkeeper and said, 'Take care of him; and whatever more you spend, when I return I will repay you.' Which of these three do you think proved to be a neighbor to the man who fell into the robbers' hands?" And he said, "The one who showed mercy toward him." Then Jesus said to him, "Go and do the same" (Luke 10:25–37 NASU).

Ye have heard that it hath been said, "Thou shalt love thy neighbor, and hate thine enemy." But I say unto you, Love your enemies, bless them that curse you, do good to them that hate you, and pray for them which despitefully use you, and persecute you; That ye may be the children of your Father which is in heaven: for he maketh the sun to rise on the evil and on the good, and sendeth rain on the just and unjust (Matthew 5:43–45 KJV. See also Romans 12:14, 17–20).

And he [*Jesus*] said unto them, Go ye into all the world, and preach the gospel to every creature. He that believeth and is baptized shall be saved; but he that believeth not shall be damned. And these signs shall follow them that believe: In my name shall they cast out devils; they shall speak with new tongues; they shall take up serpents; and if they drink any deadly thing, it shall not hurt them; they shall lay hands on the sick, and they shall recover (Mark 16:15–18 KJV).

All this newness of life is from God, who brought us back to himself through what Christ did. And God has given us the task of reconciling people to him (2 Corinthians 5:18 NLT).

END RESULT

The Kingdom Established

And from Jesus Christ, the faithful witness, the firstborn of the dead, and the ruler of the kings of the earth. To Him who loves us and released us from our sins by His blood—and He has made us {to be} a kingdom, priests to His God and Father—to Him {be} the glory and the dominion forever and ever. Amen (Revelation 1:5–6 NASU).

I WILL PUT MY LAWS INTO THEIR MINDS, AND I WILL WRITE THEM ON THEIR HEARTS. AND I WILL BE THEIR GOD, AND THEY WILL BE MY PEOPLE (Hebrews 8:10b NASU).

And they [*our brethren*] overcame him [*Satan, the devil*] because of the blood of the Lamb and because of the word of their testimony, and they did not love their life even when faced with death (Revelation 12:11 NASU).

Eternal Dwelling Place

Knowing that He who raised the Lord Jesus will raise us also with Jesus and will present us with you. For all things {are} for your sakes so that the grace which is spreading to more and more people may cause the giving of thanks to abound to the glory of God. Therefore we do not lose heart, but though our outer man is decaying, yet our inner man is being renewed day by day. For momentary, light affliction is producing for us an eternal weight of glory far beyond all comparison, while we look not at the

97

things which are seen, but at the things which are not seen; for the things which are seen are temporal, but the things which are not seen are eternal (2 Corinthians 4:14–18 NASU).

Everyone who is victorious will eat from the tree of life in the paradise of God (Revelation 2:7b NLT).

For the Lord your God has arrived to live among you. He is a mighty savior. He will rejoice over you with great gladness. With his love, he will calm all your fears. He will exult over you by singing a happy song (Zephaniah 3:17 NLT).

MY NOTES

MY NOTES

MY NOTES

MY NOTES

MY NOTES

MY NOTES

MY NOTES

AUTHOR BIOGRAPHY

Dr. Ruth's first interest in Christianity occurred as a youth, after reading a Gideon New Testament. He was deeply moved by the healing miracles of the Gospel and wondered if they occurred in modern times. He began a long, lonely search to find the relevance of the New Testament and God's will for his life. During this time, he came to realize the unprecedented position of Jesus' resurrection in the history of salvation.

Dr. Ruth's son found a copy of *Healing the Sick* by T.L. Osborne in a vacated apartment and gave it to his father. As Dr. Ruth read the book, he experienced a spiritual awakening which led to his spiritual rebirth. Shortly thereafter, he became active in a charismatic church, particularly its educational program and street witnessing outreach. His walk of faith, reflected in this handbook, is the result of intense Bible study and his desire to fulfill the Great Commission.

If you were to visit Dr. Ruth's church, you might find him blowing the shofar or ram's horn. Although not a muscial instrument, its use is cited in scripture from Genesis to Revelation. When blown in a worship service, it serves as a wake up call to worship the Lord and follow the promptings of the Holy Spirit.

Academically, Richard L. Ruth earned a doctorate in economics from the University of Wisconsin in Madison and taught for ten years in colleges and universities across the United States and Canada. He was an Economics

Department Chairman and ended his academic career with the rank of Full Professor of Economics. In the years that followed he served as a corporate economist for a Fortune 500 company in New York City. Since 1980, Dr. Ruth has been self-employed as a consulting economist based in New Jersey.

Learn more about the author's activities and becoming a living stone for Jesus, through his web site:

www.living-stones.info

INDEX